Sunny's Days

Sunny and Nana at the Park

Written and Illustrated by

Tanicca Smith

Print information available on the last page

Rev. date: 03/21/2019

To order additional copies of this book, contact:
Xlibris
1-888-795-4274
www.Xlibris.com
Orders@Xlibris.com

Sunny's Days

Sunny and Nana at the Park

Sunny and her great-grandmother Nana loved taking walks to the park. As soon as Sunny got to the park, she ran straight to the swings. Nana propped Sunny onto the swing carefully.

Now Sunny was on the seat of the swing and ready to be pushed. "ONE . . . TWO . . . THREE!" counted Sunny. "I'm ready to go," Sunny said to her great-grandmother Nana.

After being pushed several times, Sunny no longer needed her great- grandmother's help. She could swing back and forth all on her own. Sunny was a big girl. Look at Sunny's Nana—she was swinging on her own too. Nana is a big girl too!

Okay, the swing was fun, but now it was time play on something else. Sunny ran toward the big kids' slide, with her great-grandmother Nana following behind her. The slide is the next best thing at the park.

Down the slide Sunny came. Her great-grandmother Nana held her arms out to catch her. "Weeeeeeee!" said Sunny. "I love sliding down the slide. Can we do it again?"

"Of course we can do it again," said Great-Grandma Nana. "But this time, I'm going to go down the slide with you." Nana climbed the stairs of the slide, and Sunny followed after.

"Are you ready, Sunny?" asked her great-grandmother Nana. "Yes, I am," Sunny replied. Together both Sunny and her Nana came soaring down the slide.

Sunny and her great-grandmother Nana continued to play at the park for another hour.

After all of the hard playing at the park with her great-grandmother Nana, Sunny took a nice bath and went straight to sleep.

Printed in the United States
By Bookmasters